741.672

KU-546-672

r Sixth Form College
gers Hill Road
2 7EW

ESSENTIAL
FASHION
ILLUSTRATION
MEN

ESSENTIAL

FASHION
ILLUSTRATION
MEN

BEVERLY MASSACHUSETTS

ROCKPORT
PUBLISHERS

Copyright © 2008 by **maomao** publications
First published in 2008 in the United States of America by
Rockport Publishers, a member of
Quayside Publishing Group
100 Cummings Center
Suite 406-L
Beverly, MA 01915-6101
Telephone: (978) 282-9590
Fax: (978) 283-2742
www.rockpub.com

ISBN-13: 978-1-59253-505-7
ISBN-10: 1-59253-505-4

10 9 8 7 6 5 4 3 2

Publisher: Paco Asensio
Editorial coordination: Anja Llorella Oriol
Text edition: Chidy Wayne
Art director: Emma Termes Parera
Layout: Gemma Gabarron Vicente
English translation: Heather Bagott

Editorial project:
maomao publications
Tallers, 22 bis, 3º 1ª
08001 Barcelona, Spain
Tel.: +34 93 481 57 22
Fax: +34 93 317 42 08
www.maomaopublications.com

Printed in Singapore

CONTENTS

INTRODUCTION

When I received an email saying that there was a project about men's fashion illustration, for which they were counting on me, I could not believe it. Had somebody read my mind? This future book had been the one I always yearned for in my years as a fashion design student! And, until now, I had not found any that dealt with the subject.

Fashion illustration should be somewhat generic where women's and men's fashion is taken into consideration. The problem is that fashion today seems to be created exclusively for women—at least this is the feeling one gets after browsing through bookstores.

But the reality is different. The myth that men do not worry about how they dress only changing from their office suit to their casual wear is something that nowadays clashes with reality. The growing obsession regarding physique, which leads them to pack into fitness centers and use exfoliating creams, is also reflected when they are clothes shopping. The width of their garments follows the trends that the stylists praise in the magazines and they undoubtedly know three times as many fashion designers as their fathers.

Women, on the other hand, not only maintain their eternal obsession with physical beauty, but also work and run the home. Things are levelling out for both genders, which means that interests, such as fashion, are shared.

In view of the current situation, it has been decided that men's fashion should be included on the shelves of bookstores, and so we present this book of men's fashion illustrations—their faces, clothes, and poses.

In this discussion about illustration we will find certain differences between the male and the female, but this does not imply that one is better or more beautiful than the other. It is true that men do not have the stylish curves of women, but those curves are replaced by shapely muscles, which are equally attractive. And although a woman's pose is a lot more theatrical than that of a man, the latter can evoke greater strength. The important thing is that, in both fashion worlds, there should be an overriding objective when putting illustrations on paper: they must be understood.

A good illustration is usually the first step toward a successful collection, because it will be useful for all those who participate in its production process: from the sales clerk at the fabric store, to the pattern maker, to the client. And it is also useful because they all understand it and know how to translate it as though it were a language.

Bases
and Proportions

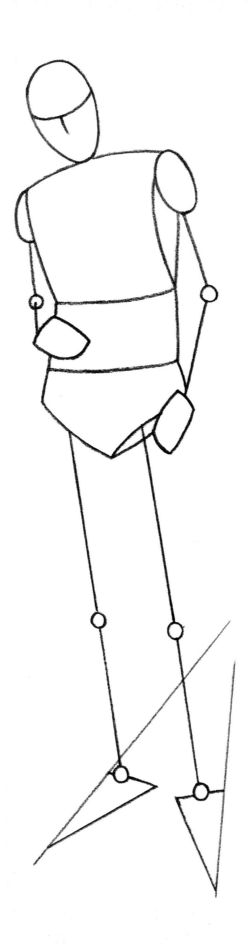

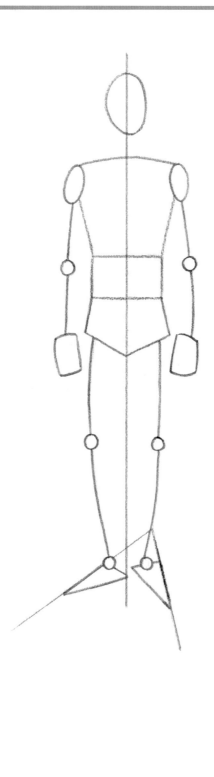

When drawing the human figure whether for a fashion illustration or not, being aware of the structures and proportions of the body is vital. One of the most popular techniques with which to start is the conversion of the figure to geometric shapes.

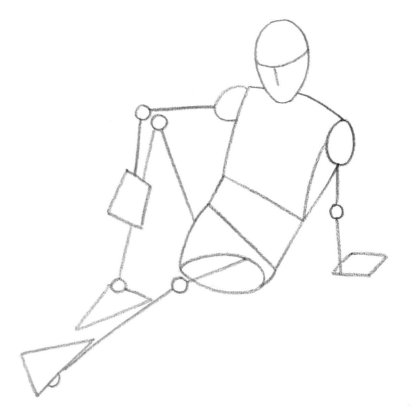

The classic proportion of the
human body is traditionally
represented as being 8 heads
tall; however, in the fashion
world where slim bodies are
the norm, 8½ heads are
preferred.

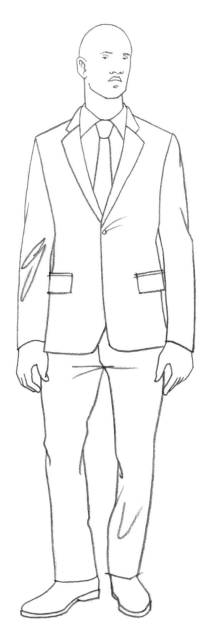

1

2

3

4

5

6

7

8

8½

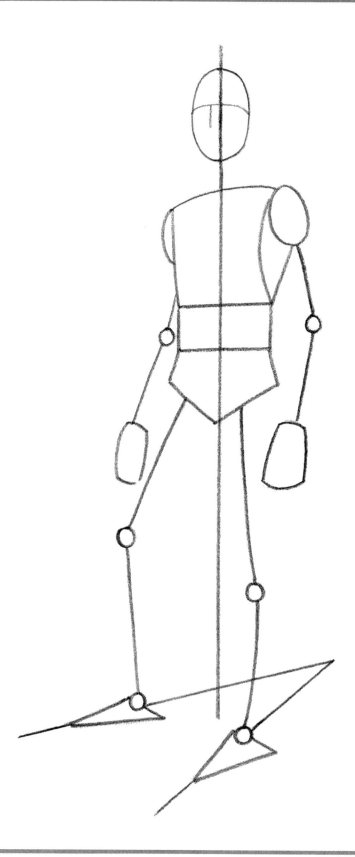

If the feet are not positioned correctly the figure loses credibility. Drawing balance lines is very useful in order to fix the figure in the space.

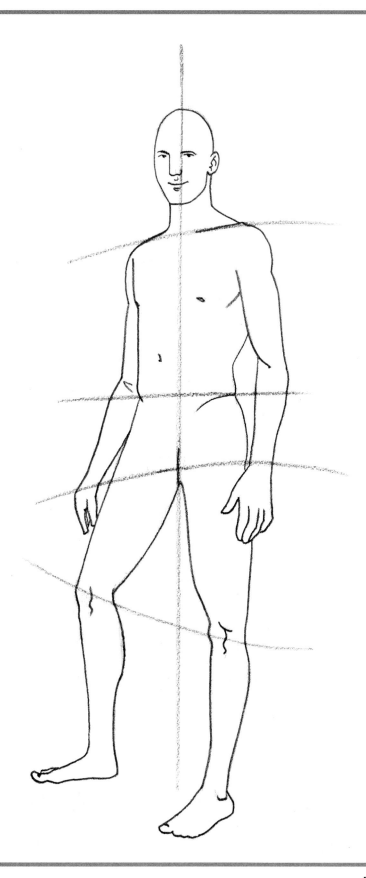

The horizontal lines that accentuate the position of the figure are those of the shoulders, waist, hips, and knees. The imaginary, flexible line stretching from the cranium to the sacrum is our vertical guide.

The head is created by joining a circular shape and an oval shape. The eyes are drawn approximately where these two shapes come together in line with the upper part of the ears.

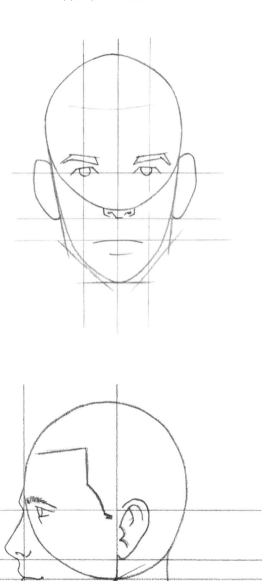

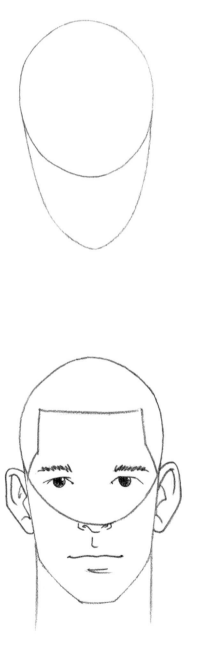

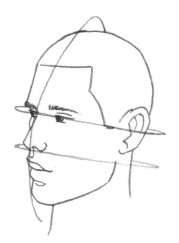

It is important that a coherent relationship between the eyes, ears, nose and mouth is maintained, regardless of the position of the head. Here are some examples of lines that can help.

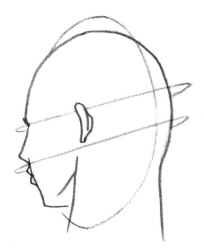

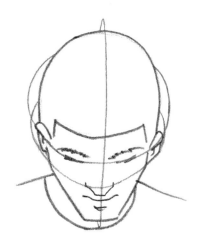

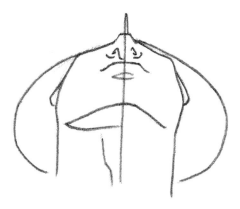

The eyes give expression and personality to the figure. When they are being drawn, it should be noted that the eyebrows are thicker towards the center. The eyelids and corners of the eyes are also important features.

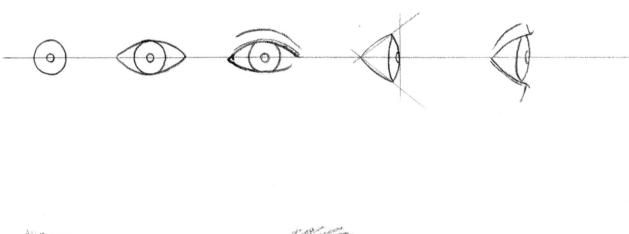

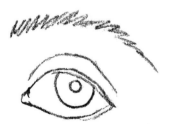

Here the drawing of the nose can be seen from different angles. The position of the nose will dictate to what degree the nostrils and the nose wings are noticeable.

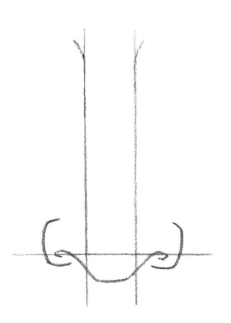

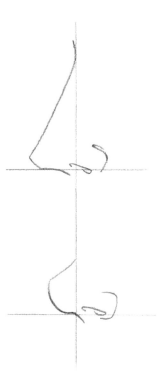

The ear has always been a problem due to its strange interior shape. Good observation can lead us to simplify certain lines, resulting in a less complex version of the ear.

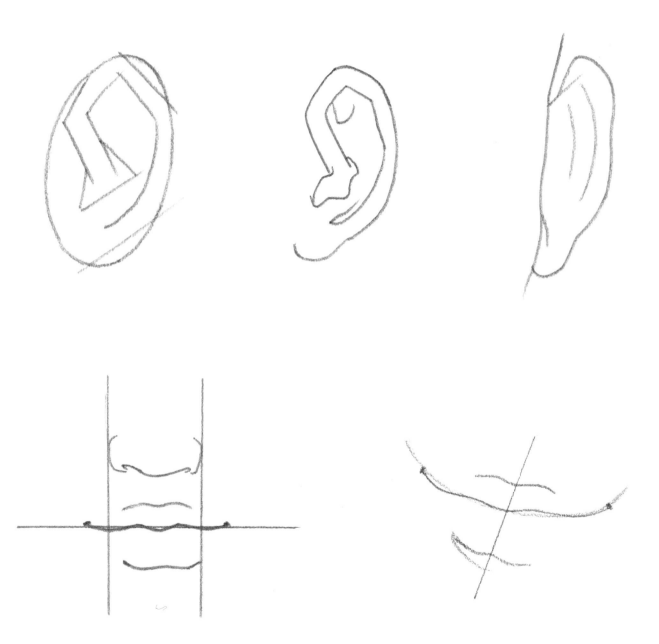

The mouth of the man is usually represented as being thinner than that of the woman. Thick lips are represented without fully completing the shape. For thin lips it is sufficient to faintly mark the bottom of the lower lip.

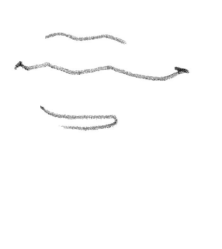

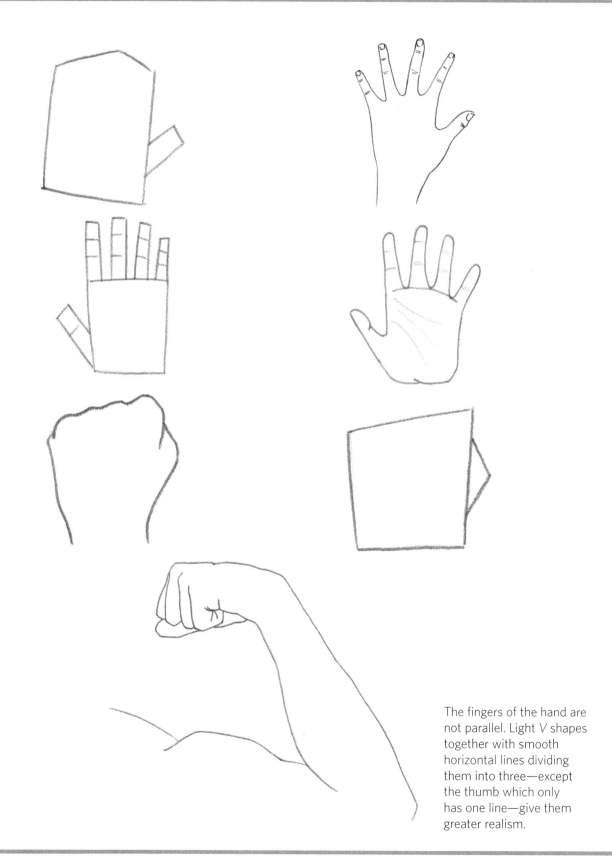

The fingers of the hand are not parallel. Light *V* shapes together with smooth horizontal lines dividing them into three—except the thumb which only has one line—give them greater realism.

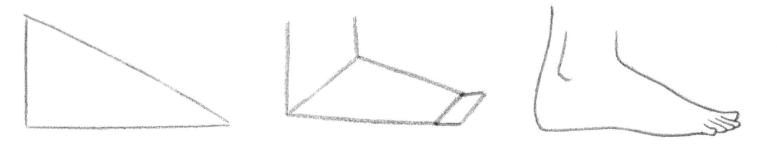

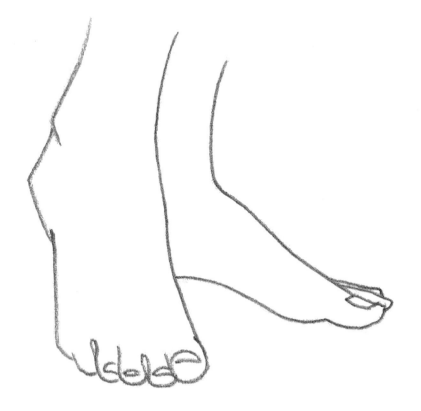

The feet are one of the most complicated parts of the human body to capture correctly. The soles and the insteps are never totally flat.

Poses

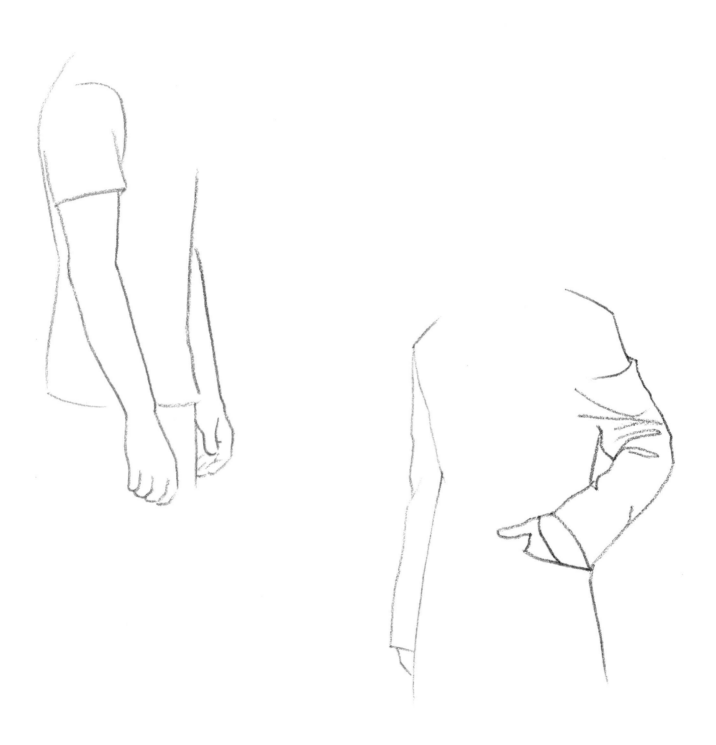

Here are some examples of arm and leg positions. The pose will directly influence the position and intensity of the creases in the sleeves.

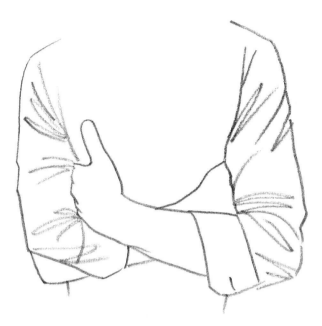

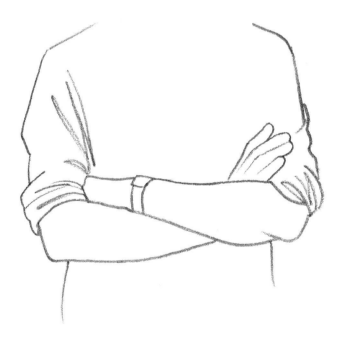

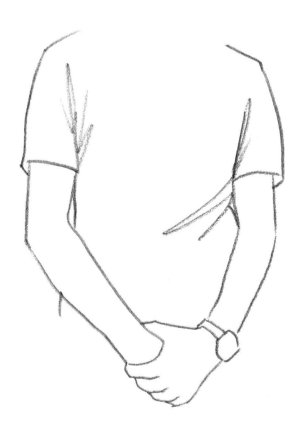

The extended arm reaches the crotch area and is never shown totally straight. In the lower illustration we can see that the right arm is foreshortened, which makes it seem smaller in accordance with the laws of perspective.

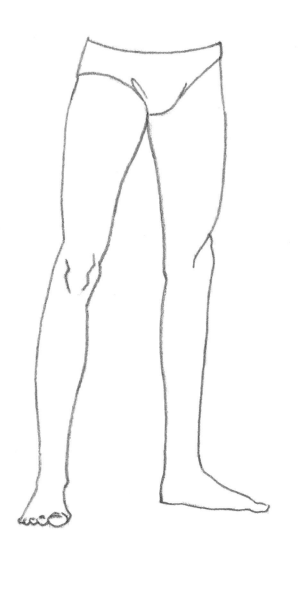

When the position is half profile one of the legs is sketched at a slightly different height in order to achieve as true a picture of the perspective as possible.

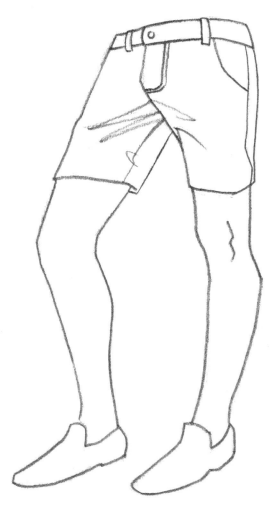

The fact that the human body does not have straight lines should be taken into account. A gentle curve would be more realistic. When drawing a profile, the position of the lower foot depends on how open the legs are.

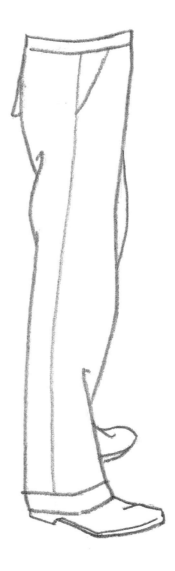

However complex the pose may be, the figure should always be balanced. Therefore the correct positioning of the feet requires careful study.

When showing movement, the back leg is the one which creates greater tension in the crease of the fly. These creases should be drawn with light strokes.

With few substantial transformations in the last century, the suit is, and will continue to be, the key piece in the masculine wardrobe. This special section will show how it is presented according to its size, material, or pattern.

Tailored suit. A classic suit confers a slightly geometric and solid look to the shoulders and chest as though it were a box or suit of armor. The tie follows the curved line of the chest.

Tight fitting suit. The shoulders and chest are still square shaped and the trousers make short creases at the seams, created by quick strokes. The right forearm, foreshortened, is close to the biceps area with an *S*-shaped crease.

Wide fitting suit. The shoulder pads protrude slightly from the shoulder creating a small fold. The trousers are shown with fewer creases that are deeper and longer.

Short trousers/long trousers. As the figures show, the shorter length trousers have hardly any creases at the bottom, whereas the trousers with a longer length create deeper creases around the ankle area.

In poses with the hands in the pockets, the suit jacket is lifted up. To portray this, arched shaped creases can be drawn. The creases formed by the trousers touching the instep are also obvious.

Here is an example of how the trousers fall in a seated position. The creases are concentrated in the crotch area where the opposing tensions stretch from the central seam of the trousers.

The material of the suit will dictate the rigidity of the suit's appearance. Wool, shown here, creates a lot of creases, although they appear soft. In the right leg, the ironing crease is not continuous when interrupted by a natural crease or fold.

A patterned suit can never be uniform. In this figure the checks act as a mesh and enable us to see how the volumes of the body are drawn and how the lines are broken by creases.

The movement of the arm when raised causes the waistcoat to follow suit, rising from the central front part. The resulting creases can be represented by *3* or *Z* shapes in a spontaneous and light fashion.

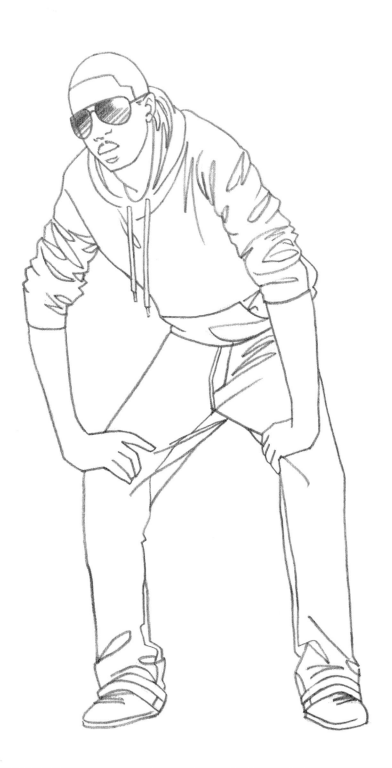

Rolled up sleeves create squashed, oval-shaped creases. Here we can see that the rise of the crotch is lower due to the trousers having a wide fitting.

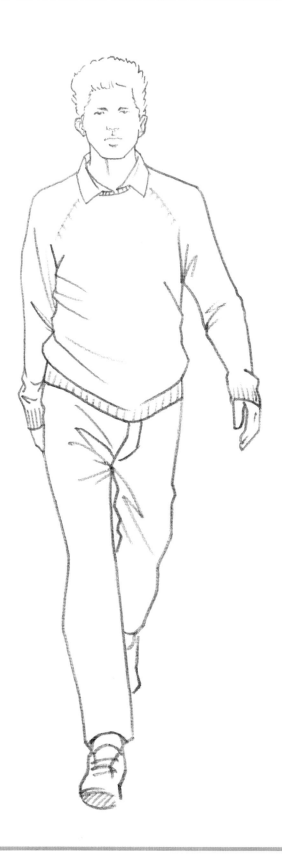

It is very important to correctly portray the creases when the figure is in movement in order to give a good picture of the garments. When walking, the main tension is produced from the hip of the front leg to the knee of the back leg.

The selected pose depends on what we want to highlight in the figure. In the example on the left, the pose represents a relaxed attitude as does the attire. With the figure on the right we want to accentuate the cummerbund.

Poses with the hands in the pockets are perfect for simplifying the drawing task or when giving the figure attitude. Here are some examples of different ways of posing in this position.

When we place hands in pockets we should always make the corresponding creases. The hand in the pocket creates different tensions depending on the pose.

A long sleeve is also affected by placing the hand in the pocket of the trousers. Touching the pocket creates creases at the bottom of the sleeve.

Views of the back are equally as precise as views of the front. Elbows, the back of the knees, and the Achilles heel are usually the starting point for many creases, without forgetting the lower part of the behind.

In this backwards-facing pose, thanks to the jumpsuit, the way the creases follow the movement of the body is seen perfectly. The man standing straight up with his back towards us is pulling on the garment from the back part of the knees.

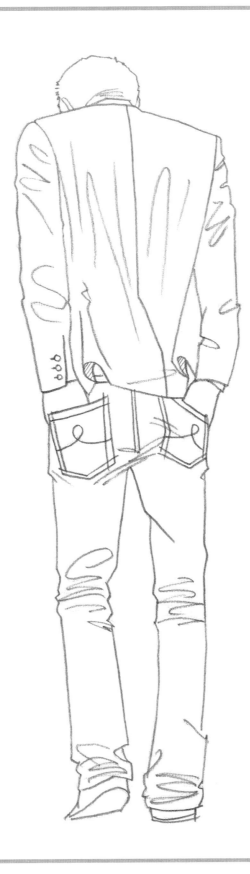

It is possible to try something different apart from the classic poses of standing, sitting, or lying down. In these cases, however, the creases will be much greater.

When presenting a collection using a group, it is important that each figure poses in a different and unique way while still maintaining the harmony of the group.

Hairstyles
and Accessories

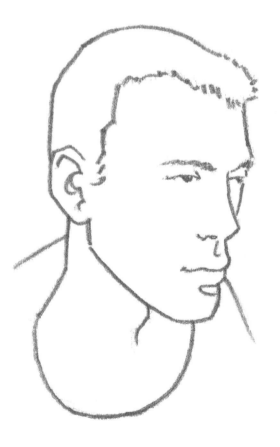

Hairstyles should be worked in the same way as creases: with a quick and firm stroke. This ensures that the lines of the hairstyle, albeit in a more simplified way, greatly resemble reality.

When the hair has loose curls, the outline should be drawn with uneven semicircles. The way to create an irregular style, as with tight curly hair, is to draw the outline with the wrong hand.

Long hair requires imagination from the illustrator. The style of the hair should be frequently different—brushed outwards, brushed inwards—and always with loose and different strokes.

Glasses are the only orthopedic object considered an element of fashion. Here we see different models: round, thick-rimmed, thick-rimmed metal, and sunglasses with a metal frame.

The reflected light of sunglasses can be shown in many ways as it is very irregular. A simple method is using white parallel lines.

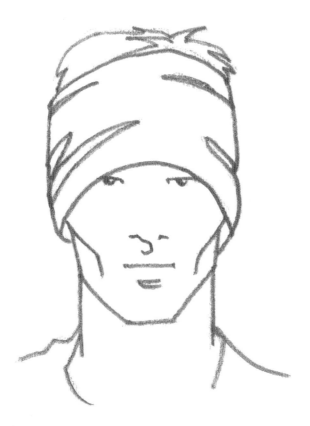

When drawing hairbands it is a good idea to apply creases which stretch from the edge to the centre. If creases are only used in the center the result is unrealistic.

When drawing visors, it should be remembered that the interior part is more shaded. This shade could be emphasized very simply.

Hoods are not easy to interpret. Their behavior is very irregular. In this example we can see how the position of the figure's head makes the hood taut from the shoulder area.

When drawing hats or caps, as in this case, it is useful to draw a little bit of hair at the sides to make the illustration more realistic.

There are many ways to knot scarves, ties, and bowties. If we have to sketch a close-up then we have to be very careful when creating the knots—where the majority of the main creases arise.

Bags for men tend to be large. The creases mostly arise from bags made of fabric—given that the leather used for bags is usually very hard and rigid.

Here we present various models of shoes seen from different angles. It is important to consider carefully the seams and laces and also understand that the heel is more attractive when shown in perspective.

These poses of feet should remind us of their importance in the drawing of a figure. As we have already said, a correct positioning of the feet is essential in giving credibility to the figure—this positioning could be innovative or more straight forward.

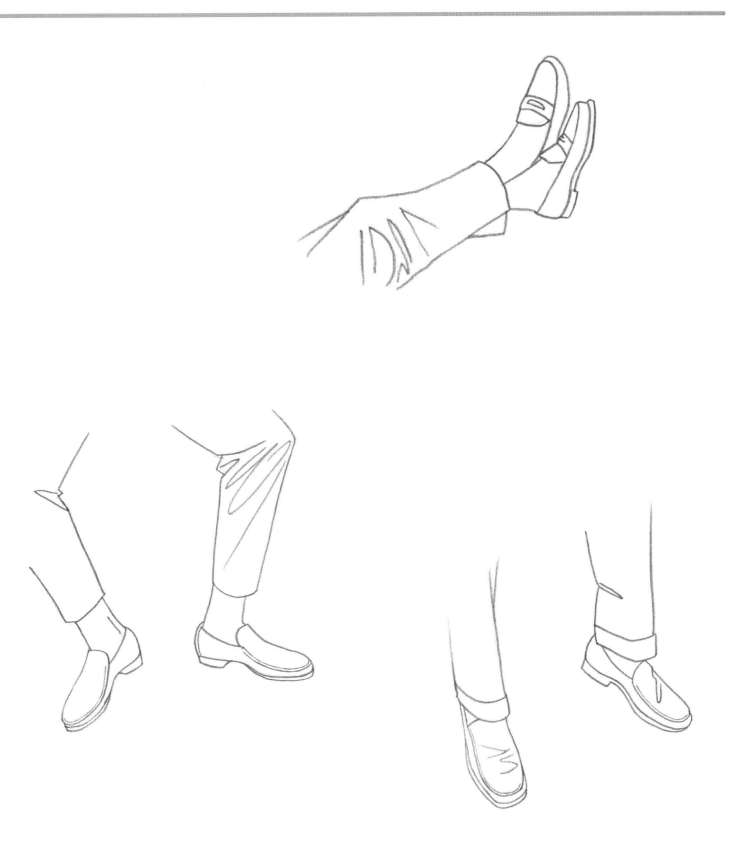

Flat
Drawing

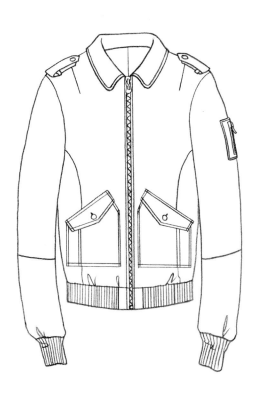

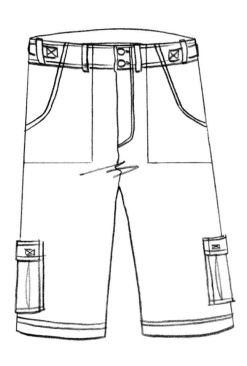

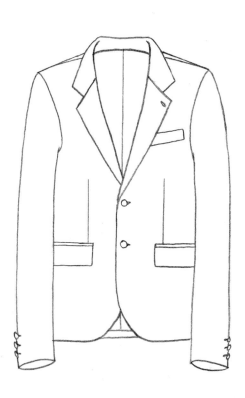

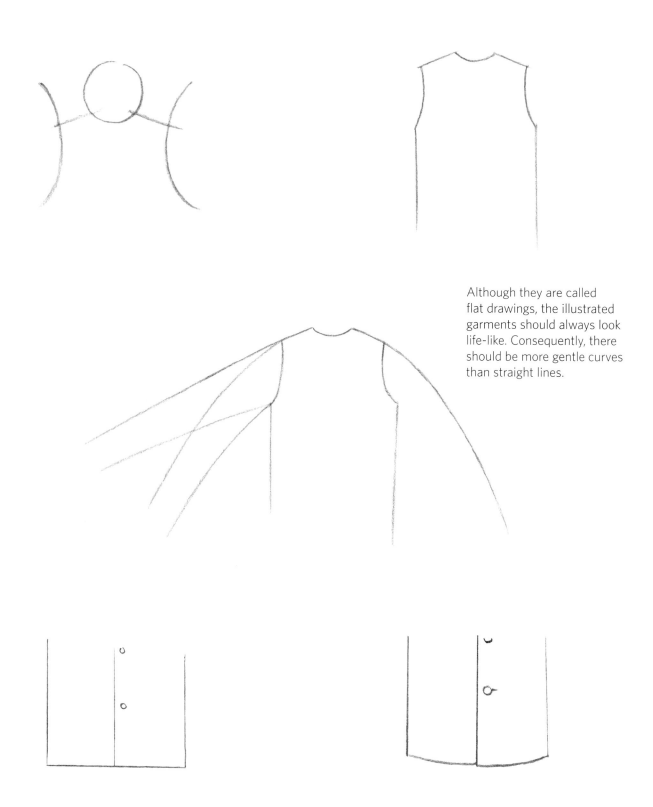

Although they are called flat drawings, the illustrated garments should always look life-like. Consequently, there should be more gentle curves than straight lines.

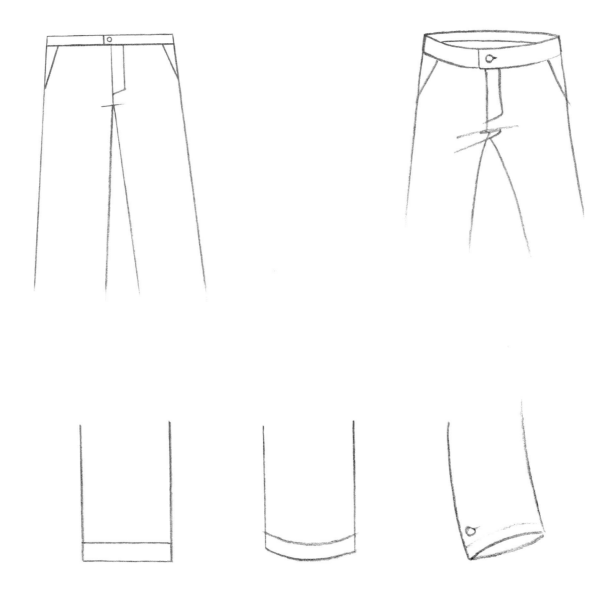

T-shirt

Polo Shirt

Long Sleeved T-shirt

Long Sleeved T-shirt Back View

The sleeves should be drawn with a curve as well as the waist, which usually tapers slightly. In the same vein, the hems should not be drawn with a straight line.

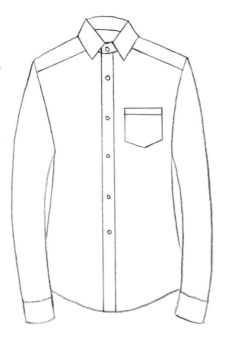

Classic Shirt

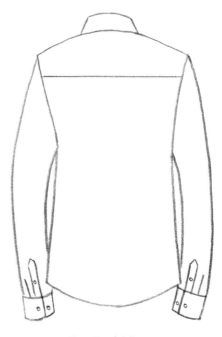

Shirt Back View

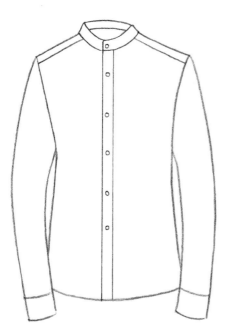

Mao Collar Shirt

Striped Pattern

Ribbed areas are illustrated by lines of varying width depending on the required thickness. Here we can see two wool jumpers: one with a thin gauge and the other with a much thicker gauge.

Djellaba Collar Shirt

V-neck Woolen Jumper

Polo Neck Jumper

Waistcoat

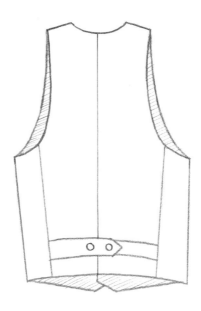

Waistcoat Back View

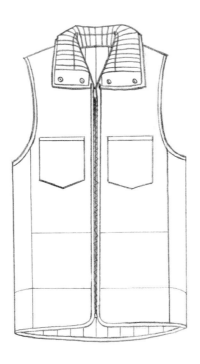

Padded Waistcoat

A flat drawing must show all the details. On this page we can see two types of waistcoat with different linings: the upper one has a normal lining and the lower one has a padded lining.

Double seams, fasteners, details. The flat drawing requires intricate detail, which calls for the use of a lead pencil or a sharp, hard pencil (H).

Empire Vest

Underpants

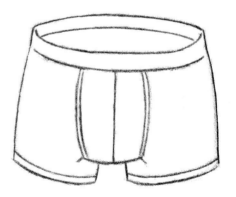

Boxer Shorts

Athletics Shorts

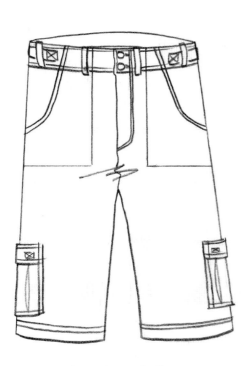

Cargo Bermuda Shorts

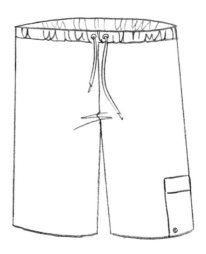

Long Length Swim Shorts

We can see here how a ribbed
elastic hem or waist affects
the predominant material of
the garment. The material is
gathered in where it reaches
the elastic, thereby altering
its size.

Tracksuit Bottoms

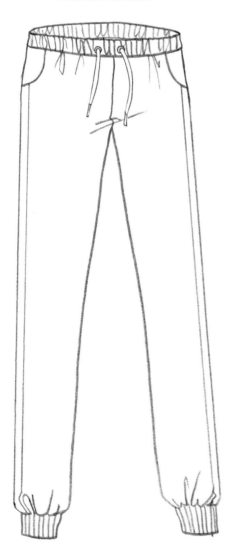

Denim Dungarees

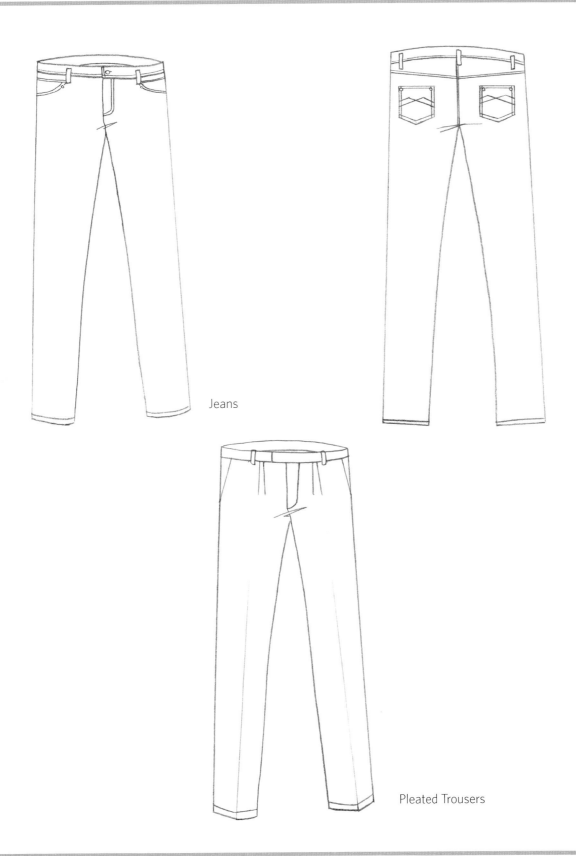

Jeans

Pleated Trousers

Tailored Jacket

Blazer

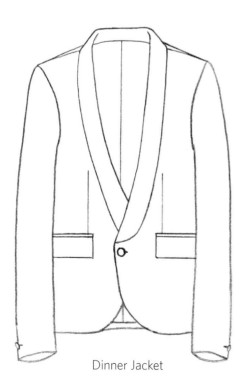

Dinner Jacket

Morning Coat

The button holes, lapels,
lining, pocket flaps, and pleats
on a single jacket, as with
any other garment, must be
drawn. This is the job of the
flat drawing—to make the
garment fully comprehensible.

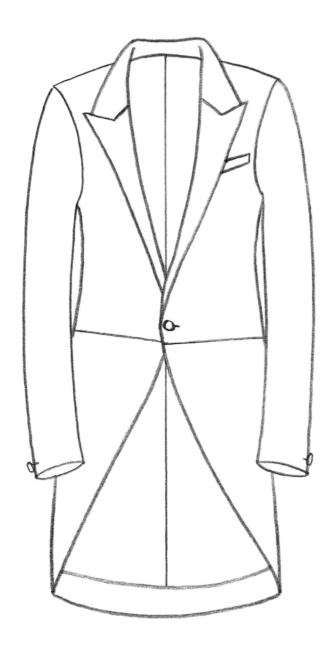

Morning Suit

A flat drawing is successful when the garment it depicts is clearly understood. This type of drawing is what is shown to the person who will produce to these specifications.

Hooded Sweatshirt

Wind Breaker

Jacket

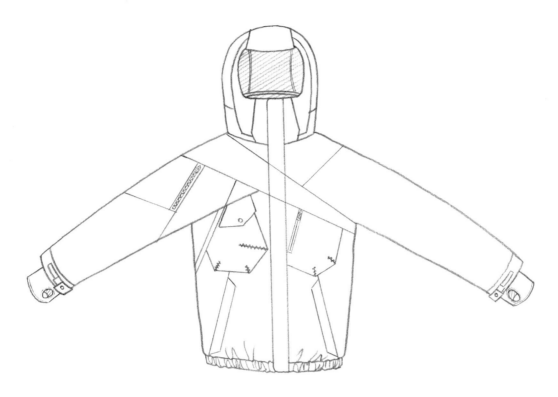

Ski Jacket

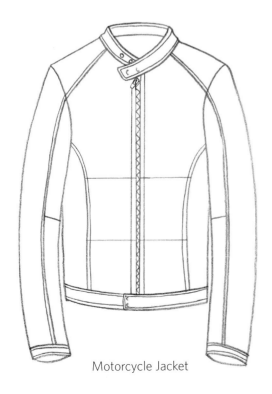

Motorcycle Jacket

Anorak

Long Length Coat

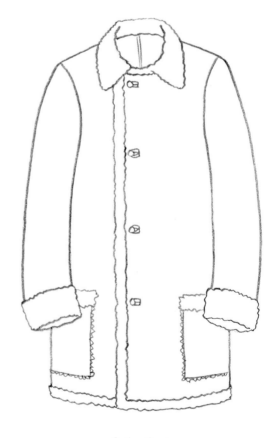

Sailor Coat

Generally there are not many creases in flat drawings; however, they can be included when drawing a garment with a belt to draw attention to it and show it as a separate piece.

Parka

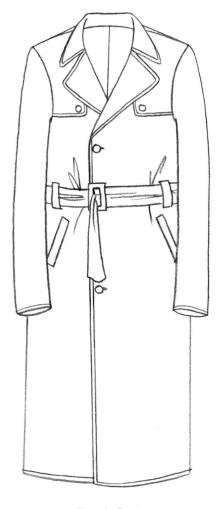

Trench Coat

Illustrating with Pencil, Colored Pencil, and Crayon

The pencil is the best tool with which to sketch, as it is erasable and is ideal for modifying when we are not certain what we want to draw.

In these figures we are using very soft pencils (B) with an unsharpened lead. We would use this tool for sketches that do not require much detail.

The use of very thick pencils enables the figure to be sensed by intuition as some areas are left unsketched. This is the case with the legs in this figure where the continuity is sensed even though we have not completed the outline.

Here, we use a pencil that
is slightly thinner than the
previous one although it is
equally soft. With this pencil,
details such as buttons or
specific creases can be added
to the drawing.

Normally, the soft pencil (B) gives a more attractive finish on porous paper. The result is always more artistic and gratifying.

From this point onwards we will work with normal pencils, which are also soft, and allow us to work in greater detail and bring the faces to life.

To give credibility to a look and soul to a figure, the shine in the eyes must be positioned correctly. The interior corners of the eyes and eyelids must also be taken into account—as we saw in the first part.

With a lead pencil (0.5) we can take the detail to another level. It is an ideal tool for drawing double seams, thin ribs, patterns, strings, etc.

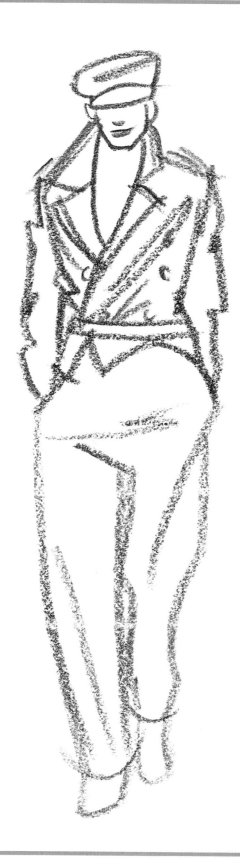

The color pencil is usually soft and allows us to outline in such a way that the color forms part of the interior. We can also color in the garment and outline the details with a different color to mark the difference.

When we use color we do not have to color in the whole area. We can leave some spaces in white. These would represent the more illuminated areas of the garment.

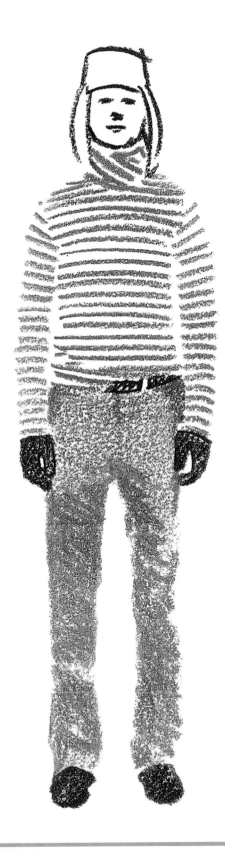

When we create illustrations with patterned material we can omit the figure outline. The pattern itself creates its own limits, thereby giving a misleading sense of continuity.

When coloring in with pencil, the only thing to remember is that creases have to be darker. This is the only way they can be distinguished from the rest of the garment.

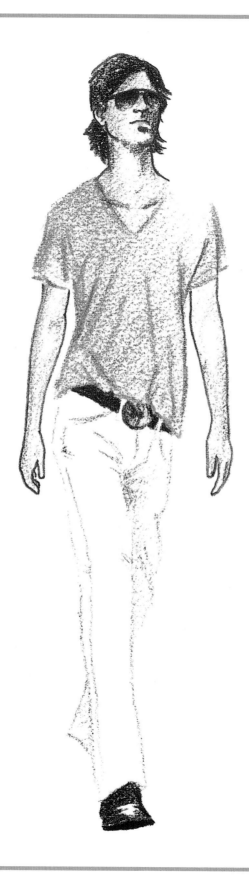

Shaded areas do not always have to be grey or black. Sometimes it is preferable to apply shading with complementary colors, such as blue or violet on the skin.

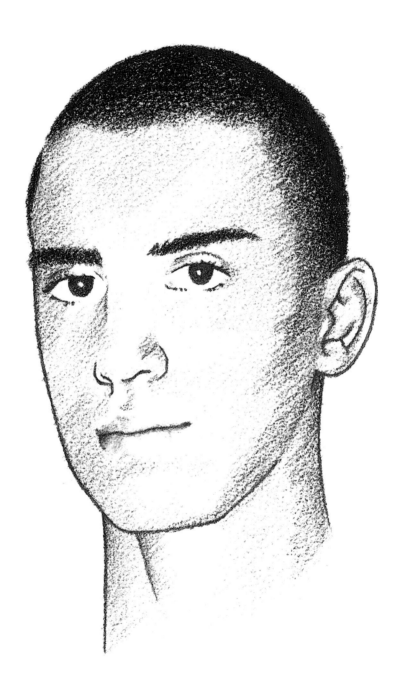

Crayons are very waxy so they are not usually suited to detailed work. They should be used with light strokes so that the surface of the drawing does not get sticky.

It is a good idea to use a fixing spray when the illustration is finished, since greasiness could stain other drawings when they are stored.

If we are quick and have a steady hand then crayons are a good tool with which to draw silhouettes. It is important to bear in mind that work cannot be erased if an error is made.

Given the lack of precision crayons offer, we will use them in a very limited way when sketching. Here, the details should not be the most important feature.

Crayons are great for filling in large areas. If we crayon on top of a photograph we can achieve a very real effect. Here, cotton wool has been used to blur the image.

Illustrating with Felt-Tip Pen

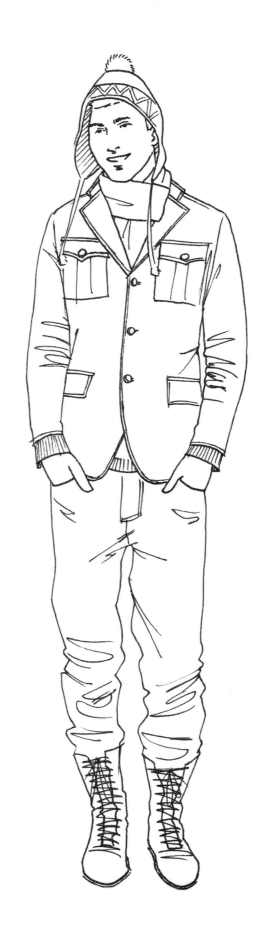

Felt-tip pens are very good tools for advanced illustrators. The result is clean and aesthetically pleasing as long as the brush strokes are quick and sure.

As with the pencil, medium sized felt-tip pens (1.2 mm) give a high level of detail that is ideal for faces, creases, accessories, and fasteners.

As we can see in these illustrations, the medium felt-tip pen, as well as the thick one, should be used with care to draw faces. A simplification of the features is the best solution.

To completely fill in a figure with a felt-tip pen requires previous study. It is advisable to fill in whole parts (sleeves, necks, trouser legs, etc.) in one go from the top to the bottom and then carefully give them a deeper shade.

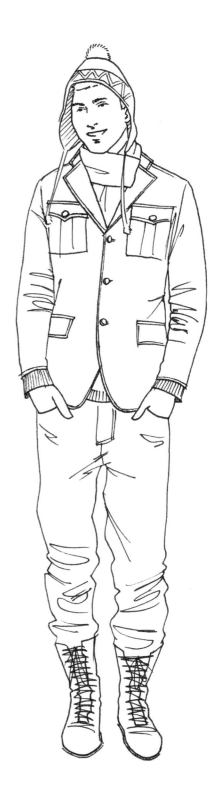

The fine 0.4 mm felt-tip pen
will be the one used to bring
out details as much as possible.
With this type of felt-tip pen
it is possible to draw almost
any kind of detail.

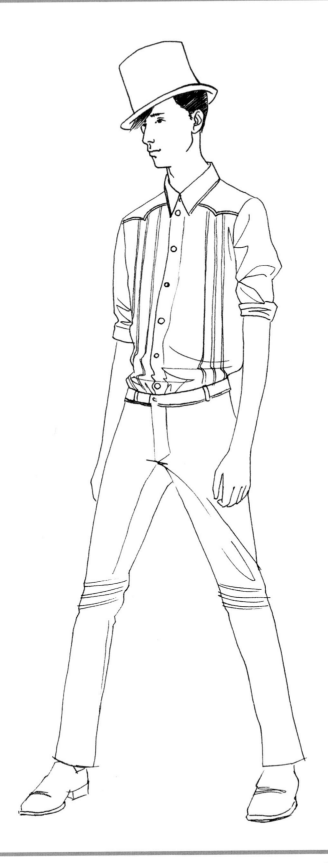

With color felt-tip pens we can greatly simplify the figure, filling in only those zones which correspond to shade. The human eye allows us to imagine the rest of the figure.

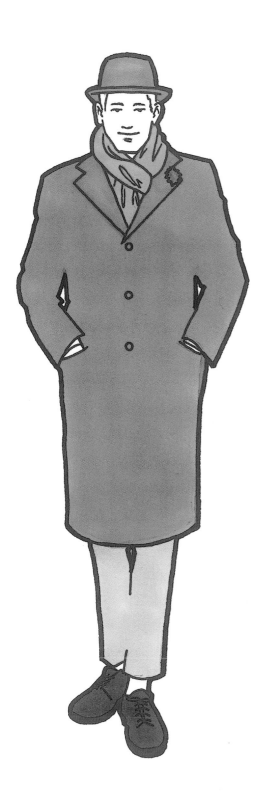

We can use the felt-tip pen throughout to create a flat drawing, or by using it another way we can leave areas blank to give a shiny effect.

To draw creases on a color once we have completed the figure, we can mark them with the same color, albeit a slightly deeper shade, so that they are distinguishable.

It is important to remember that the lines on striped patterns should not be drawn straight. These lines follow the movement of the body and so become broken when confronted by pronounced creases.

For patterns in general it
is not necessary to draw
them completely. We can
draw some areas and leave
others to the imagination.
This technique creates a
false sensation of volume.

Illustrating with
Ink and Watercolor

Ink fills all spaces perfectly. By leaving quite a few blank spaces for the creases, we can create the desired shiny finish.

If the ink is greatly watered down it is difficult to predict its behavior. One way to safeguard a good outline is to use sticky tape around the edge so that the ink can be used freely. Once the ink is dry the sticky tape can be carefully removed.

In the illustration on the right we wanted to show a pair of trousers in different shades—achievable by using a very weak water-color and a mix of colors.

Watercolor is an ideal medium for interpreting transparencies. We simply color the texture under the fabric and once this is dry, a second watered-down layer is applied on top.

A sucessful watercolor drawing is achieved from a good base in pencil. When we want to create stronger outlines, the use of pencil will result in greater definition.

With watercolor and a skilled hand we can achieve very realistic results. To lighten areas once the surface has been painted, water from the moist drawing can be absorbed by cellulose paper.

The shaded areas will
be applied once we have
completed the first base
color. The result will
depend on how long
the first layer is allowed
to dry.

Voluminous hair is achieved with a pale and irregular layer of watercolor first. Once this is dry we continue with light brushstrokes applying a darker color.

We can outline the figure in black to emphasize the illustration. This was done with great mastery by René Gruau, possibly the best fashion illustrator of the twentieth century.

Combining watercolor with another tool, such as a pencil or felt tip pen, to draw the outline of the figure allows us to use the watercolor splashes quickly and with a very artistic result.

A combination of techniques is always welcome. It can help us to emphasize shaded areas, highlight creases, or simply outline a figure.

Watercolor easily enables us to leave plenty of blank spaces. Light and shadow must be taken into account for the effect to be natural.

In these kinds of illustrations the result would be imprecise if only watercolor were used. A better result is achieved by going around the outline with a felt tip pen.

Here is a further example of a combination of illustration techniques. When details or outlines of the same color in felt tip pen are applied to a watercolor base the result is greatly enhanced.

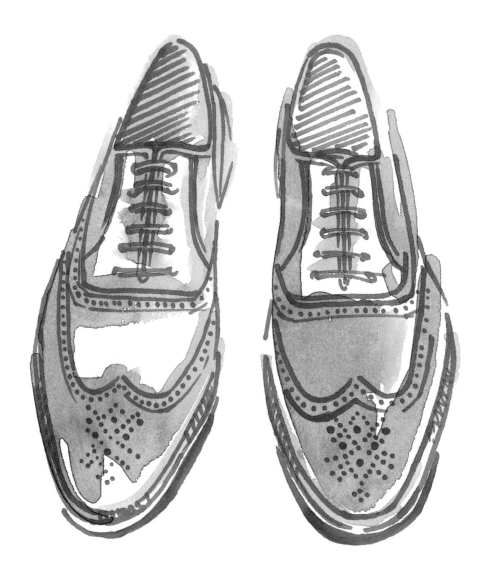

If a background is desired then irregular splashes of watercolor can be used. This works very well, as we can see here, where the figure has been colored in while leaving a lot of blank areas.